Sun Tzu's

ART *of* WAR
FOR TRADERS
AND INVESTORS

Sun Tzu's

ART of WAR FOR TRADERS AND INVESTORS

Dean Lundell

McGraw-Hill

New York   San Francisco   Washington, D.C.   Auckland   Bogotá
Caracas   Lisbon   London   Madrid   Mexico City   Milan
Montreal   New Delhi   San Juan   Singapore   Sydney   Tokyo   Toronto

Library of Congress Cataloging-in-Publication Data

Lundell, Dean.
    Sun Tzu's Art of war for traders and investors / Dean Lundell.
       p. cm.
    ISBN 0-07-039141-6
    1. Investments.   2. Stock exchanges.   3. Sun-tzu, 6th cent. B.C.
Sun-tzu ping fa.   I. Title.
HG4515.L86   1997
332.6—dc21
                                96-52325
                                    CIP

McGraw-Hill

A Division of The *McGraw-Hill* Companies

123456789   DOC/DOC   90210987

ISBN 0-07-039141-6

The sponsoring editors for this book were David Conti and Allyson Arias, the editing supervisor was Patricia V. Amoroso, and the production supervisor was Suzanne W. B. Rapcavage. It was designed by Michael Mendelsohn and set in Hiroshige Book by MM Design 2000, Inc.

Printed and bound by R. R. Donnelley & Sons Company.

This publication is designed to provide accurate and authoritative information in regard to the subject matter covered. It is sold with the understanding that the publisher is not engaged in rendering legal, accounting, or other professional service. If legal advice or other expert assistance is required, the services of a competent professional person should be sought.

—From a declaration of principles jointly adopted by a committee of the American Bar Association and a committee of publishers.

This book is printed on recycled, acid-free paper
containing a minimum of 50% recycled, de-inked fiber.

McGraw-Hill books are available at special quantity discounts to use as premiums and sales promotions, or for use in corporate training programs. For more information, please write to the Director of Special Sales, McGraw-Hill, 11 West 19th Street, New York, NY 10011. Or contact your local bookstore.

CONTENTS

INTRODUCTION

In my 20 years on Wall Street as an investment professional, I have read many books on investing and trading, from the rudimentary texts for beginners, to the highly sophisticated math- and computer-intensive methods for professionals. Yet nothing I read represented the basic conflict that transpires in our markets every day.

The markets are indeed in conflict. In whatever market you choose, it is perennially in conflict. It never stops: 24 hours a day, 7 days a week, information is disseminated and exchanged; perceptions are made and opinions are formed. Those opinions are then acted upon and the conflict continues. Whether it be the world's equity markets, debt markets, commodity markets, or currency markets, of one thing you can be sure: There will be winners and there will be losers.

Free markets are the last bastion of unabashed conflict. There are no government quotas, no regulations as to how much you can win or lose. The markets do not care what race you are, what religion, what color or creed, and they do not take prisoners. To participate in this conflict, you must become a soldier. In fact, you must be your own general. You must gather information, adapt to the situation at hand, devise a strategy, and execute your plan. Either you win or you lose; it is that simple.

If indeed the markets are a microcosm of conflict, with the flow of battle raging as the tide of battle turns, would not a good general be constantly evaluating the battle and have the flexibility to outflank the opponent? Of course; and so must you.

In this battle or conflict that we call free and open markets, the roster of soldiers or participants is large, diverse, and global and has distinctly different goals, objectives, and time parameters. Market participants also have a wide variance of financial means. The fascinating part of this battle is that we all occupy the same space at the same time. What role do you play? Are you trading billions of dollars, deutsche marks, or yen for a proprietary trading firm? A huge hedge fund or mutual fund? Perhaps you manage portfolios at a trust department. Or perhaps you are an individual trader or on the floor of an exchange. What role you play in this conflict will determine your methods of doing battle. One of the more intriguing aspects of this book is that although a particular concept may not apply to you, knowing that it applies to others will in fact help you defend your position or help you take advantage of a market development.

The Art of War was compiled approximately 2500 years ago, in the sixth century B.C., from the teachings of Sun Tzu, a Chinese general and philosopher. His concepts and methods have been studied and practiced for tens of centuries in Asia. His work is required reading at our military academies and, in more recent times, can be found in corporate boardrooms.

WHY I WROTE THIS BOOK

When I first read *The Art of War*, I was amazed at how after 2500 years, Sun Tzu's wisdom and concepts could be used for success in battle in the world's markets. What's more, they are not difficult to understand or implement. One just has to recognize the appropriate situation or development and apply the concept. Personally, I have changed the way I view and participate in the markets because of Sun Tzu's writings and have done so quite successfully.

The basic concept behind Sun Tzu's teachings is to win without having to fight. As contradictory as that sounds, it will become clear as you read through these passages. By being flexible and constantly adapting to ever-changing markets and events, you will find yourself in harmony with the markets so you do not have to fight.

AN OVERVIEW OF THE BOOK

The Art of War contains 13 chapters, as does this volume. Since these are a series of teachings or lessons, there actually is not a story to follow. However, you will notice that there is a logical order to them. In the first chapter, Sun Tzu asks us to consider the big picture, to look at the impending battle from a strategic perspective. From that point, he brings us to tactical considerations and finally to pragmatic ones. I have endeavored to do the same: to bring you from considering central bank policy and macroeconomics to estimating where panic buying or selling will happen and to locate the optimum place for trade execution.

What makes this book different from any other text is that it ranges beyond the traditional Sun Tzu translations to discuss how traders, be it novices or professionals, can use successful military strategies to enhance their trading and succeed in the markets. Specifically, the chapters examine and parallel the 13 chapters in the classic Sun Tzu text.

I hope you find these teachings helpful in your personal and professional life; they have inevitably enriched mine.

ACKNOWLEDGMENTS

TO SUN TZU: FOR HIS WISDOM AND INSIGHT

TO CAO CAO: FOR RECORDING SUN TZU'S TEACHINGS
FOR US

TO LIONEL GILES: FOR HIS TRANSLATION OF *THE ART OF WAR*
INTO ENGLISH IN 1910

TO MICHAEL COOGAN: FOR HAVING ME SHARE THIS WITH THE
REST OF THE WORLD

TO MY WIFE ELLEN: FOR A LIFETIME OF LOVE AND
COMMITMENT

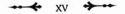

Sun Tzu's

ART *of* WAR
FOR TRADERS
AND INVESTORS

CHAPTER ONE

STRATEGIC APPRAISAL

UNDERSTANDING THE BIG PICTURE

Sun Tzu said

....

that war, or military action, is of vital importance to the nation or state. It is a matter of survival, of life and death, safety or ruin. Therefore we must study it and understand it.

Indeed, the world is changing rapidly and dramatically. While nations still exist, we no longer have a national economy; we have a global economic system and it is imperative to understand that. You must examine every aspect of this system to be successful in it.

Think of our global economic system as an ocean of assets. If a storm is raging in one locality, a calm will be in another. Where would you take your ship? Is the wind in your sails? Or are you adrift? Will the swell you are riding crash you upon the rocks?

It is essential that you understand our economic system from a global perspective in order to profit from it. You must be cognitive of central bank policy, liberal or conservative governments, economic performance, relative currency valuations, and interest rates.

In practically every country in the world, there is an equity market and a debt market. Commodities are produced and traded on a global scale and can be paid for in dollars or deutsche marks, Swiss francs or French, yen or pounds, or any number of other currencies.

Of one thing you can be sure: Like soldiers in battle, money will leave a bad market and follow a good one. It is therefore incumbent upon you to make a strategic assessment.

Sun Tzu said

that war, or conflict, is to be measured five ways: the way, the weather, the terrain, the leadership, and discipline.

Sun Tzu also said the way, or law, causes people to be in agreement with their leaders, so that they will follow without regard to danger.

The way can have a double meaning for you and me. Which way is your market clearly going and are you fighting the tape or bucking the trend? Or are money and people blindly following a "hot" market?

I have seen many traders and investors not only fail to assess the market; but then exacerbate the error by refusing to admit that they were wrong. "The market is wrong," they say. The fact is, the market is never wrong. Only we are wrong for failing to assess it properly.

The grain markets of 1995 and 1996 come to mind when I see people blindly following a hot market. A number of people who had absolutely no business trading in commodities told me that corn or wheat was the place to be. This is a classic example of people blindly following a market.

Sun Tzu said ....

the weather, or heaven, means times or seasons.

Which stage is your market in? Hope, greed, fear, or despair? What can you do about it?

These market stages are certainly no secret, but it is amazing how many traders and investors fail to recognize and assess the stages, and to make plans to protect themselves, or to take advantage of an opportunity.

The best example I can think of is the movement of technical stocks in recent years. First, people bought them with grand hopes. They saw them rise to incredible prices but became greedy and held on for more. When the stocks started to trade down in price, people were fearful but still held on. Finally, when the pain of further loss came about, they despaired, capitulated, and sold—at prices nowhere near where they had been.

Admittedly, hindsight is always 20-20, but there are techniques we can use to protect profits or at least mitigate disaster. These are addressed in later chapters.

Sun Tzu said ....

the terrain or earth means to assess the situation in terms of

time, distance, ease of travel, and danger.

What type of market are you in? Is it trending or cycling? How far can it go and in what time parameters? How volatile or dangerous is it? Or is it easy to join a trending market?

The U.S. stock market, at least in terms of the broad market averages, is a classic example of a trending market during the early 1990s. Day after day, more money poured into the market and prices were bid up proportionately. This market was easy. There actually were more mutual funds than the stocks that comprised them. Investors had only to buy them and keep on buying to make money.

As this market rose higher and higher, the volatility increased as well. Hope, greed, fear, and despair manifested themselves to such an extent that, as of this writing, the New York Stock Exchange has imposed trading curbs 87 times.

After its dramatic rise, the U.S. stock market went through a period of cycling. It would trade up to a previous high and, as sellers flooded in, would trade down to a level where enough buyers came in to support prices. The aforementioned volatility certainly contributed to that cycling period.

Sun Tzu said ....

leadership in war means courage, trustworthiness, and wisdom.

To us, it means: What is leading the market? Is debt leading equity? Is your currency, relative to others, preceding moves in your debt? Or is it commodity prices?

One of the concepts you must learn to deal with is that nothing happens in a vacuum. Events in one market will affect another. Commodity prices can affect interest rates that in turn affect stock prices. Declining prices on the Japanese stock market have a direct impact on the capital of Japanese banks, and any change will have an affect on their ability to acquire or dispose of assets—U.S. Treasury bonds, for example.

Sun Tzu said ....

that discipline means the chain of command and disposition

of resources.

For the trader or investor, discipline means to exercise good and prudent money management and risk management.

Sun Tzu said that the general who follows these principles will be victorious, and so shall you.

Sun Tzu said

that all warfare is based on deception. If strong, pretend to be weak and hold out a carrot to entice your enemy. If your opponent is superior, evade him.

This advice depends on your point of view. Let's say you are a major participant in the currency markets. You think a particular western European currency is going to decline relative to the U.S. dollar. Thus, you quietly establish a short position in the spot forward market. Once it starts to move, you make a highly visible selling campaign in the futures market. You know word will quickly spread that you are selling and others will follow, thus helping drive the market for you. Then of course you quietly reverse the transaction as others follow your lead. If, on the other hand, you happen to be an individual trader, you must be aware of this scenario.

In summary, Sun Tzu said that the general who does many calculations at headquarters will win and the one who makes few will lose. So it is with the individual trader or investor: Only by making a strategic assessment of the factors that affect your market will you win.

CHAPTER TWO

CONFLICT
TRADING AND TIMING

Sun Tzu said ....

that when armies engage in actual fighting, if victory is long in

coming, the men's weapons will become dull and their enthu-

siasm will wane.

This is particularly true for the professional trader but is also applicable to individual investors who have become desperate to make up for a loss. Do not overtrade. If you trade for a long time, you will lose the edge and start taking chances and foolish risks. The inevitable result will be a string of losing trades.

Sun Tzu said

that if you lay siege to a town, you will exhaust your strength and resources. Therefore, feed off your enemies and forage for their resources.

A more common and modern analogy is to a baseball game. How is the game won? By hitting numerous singles, not by trying for a home run. Therefore, it is better to make a few ticks or an eighth of a point on numerous trades than to bet on a big win. If you try for that big winner and you lose, your account equity will be gone and you will be out of business. Thus, it is better to conserve your resources and use them wisely. Employ prudent money and risk management.

Sun Tzu tells us ....

that the wise general not only feeds off the enemy but rewards

his soldiers with the spoils of victory.

Since you are your own general, reward yourself. After you are victorious, call your brokerage or clearing firm and ask to be sent a check. By rewarding yourself, you will reinforce a winning attitude and state of mind.

Sun Tzu reminds us ....

that the important thing is victory, not persistence.

Work smart as opposed to hard or for a long time. Consistently take profits regardless of size and increase your account equity and reward.

CHAPTER THREE

PLANNING ATTACK

DESIGNING YOUR TRADING PLAN

Sun Tzu said ....

that it is best to take the enemy's country whole and intact. It is better to capture an army than destroy it, to capture a regiment or a company than destroy it.

Sun Tzu reiterates that the most skillful tactic is to thwart the enemy's plans. The next best is to attack the enemy's army, and the worst policy is to mount a siege of a walled city. He goes on to say that if an impatient general besieges a walled city, he will lose a third of his troops.

This concept is particularly aimed at major market participants, although it is beneficial for small traders to recognize when it is happening. On occasion, major market participants will have opposing views. Typically, one will mount a major sell campaign while another will do the same on the buy side. This makes for particularly volatile markets. The battle will rage until one capitulates. Regardless of who winds up being right, both will end up devoting tremendous resources to this battle. So even the winner will sustain what could be viewed as major casualties or collateral damage.

Sun Tzu's point is that you should use superior positioning and planning rather than outright attack and battle. Thus, if you were a small individual trader caught in the middle, what would you do? Think like a guerrilla soldier: If you were in the middle of two warring armies, the best strategy would be to wait and recognize when one side is capitulating and then join the winning side. That way you can reap the spoils of victory without having to take part in the major battle.

Sun Tzu said

that he who knows when to fight and when to retreat will see victory. He who knows how to handle both superior and inferior forces will win. He will win who is prepared when attacking the unprepared. He will win whose army is motivated by the same goal. Victory will be seen by that army that is not constrained by civilian leadership.

As an individual trader or investor, you must make up your own mind whether to join the battle or stand aside until it is over. If you are joining the battle, choose sides carefully and limit the amount of resources you are willing to commit. It is better to plan ahead and anticipate when others will join the battle to turn the tide of the conflict. You know that if your market breaches a particular price level, others will be prompted to join the fray and turn the tide so the opposing side capitulates. Focus on the overall goal of why you are involved in this market in the first place.

Sun Tzu concludes

this lesson by saying that if you know yourself and your

enemy, you will not fear battle. If you know yourself but not

your enemy, you will lose a battle for every one that you win;

and if you do not know yourself and do not know your

enemy, you will never see victory.

If you know your capabilities and your market, you will be a consistent winner. If you know your capabilities and do not know your market, you will win one and lose one. At best you will break even. If you do not know your capabilities and do not know the market you are involved in, you will be a consistent loser.

CHAPTER FOUR

TACTICAL CONSIDERATIONS

REMAINING GROUNDED IN A VOLATILE ENVIRONMENT

Sun Tzu said ....

that the good warriors of old first put themselves beyond the possibility of defeat and then waited for an opportunity to defeat the enemy. Thus, the good fighter can secure himself against defeat but cannot be certain of defeating the enemy.

Sun Tzu goes on to remind us that the power to secure ourselves against defeat lies in our own hands.

We as traders or investors cannot control the market, only what we do in the market. We can discern victory, or how to make that victory possible, but we cannot manufacture it. Remember from Chapter One that we must assess the strategic picture first. We cannot cause changes in that strategic picture, but we can make plans for action given a change in it.

I can recall a largely anticipated cut in the Lombard rate by the Bundesbank. Prior to that the deutsche mark had declined rather precipitously against the U.S. dollar. When the Bundesbank did in fact lower rates, the deutsche mark actually rose in value against the U.S. dollar.

You cannot cause the Bundesbank to change interest rates. However, given the fact that the market had anticipated and discounted a lowering in those rates, you would know that those who were short deutsche marks would be buying them back and a rally would ensue. Your strategy would be to wait in ambush and be ready to buy, to force the short sellers to buy back quickly and help drive your position.

Since you cannot cause changes in strategic situations, your task is to form a tactical battle plan on the basis of whatever changes might happen in that strategic picture.

Sun Tzu said ....

that defense is for times of insufficient strength and offense is

for times of great strength.

There are a number of ways to interpret Sun Tzu's words. If you are a small trader or investor, you cannot do battle or confront major market participants. In this case it is better to trade with them. Additionally, for the individual trader, it is better to take the high-probability trade than try to lead or outguess the market.

Make use of defensive measures such as options, futures, and other hedge vehicles if you are so inclined. Use protective stop loss orders; it is better to take a small loss at first than a large one later. Live to fight another day. Never put good money after bad. As your trade or investment starts to work for you and you gather strength, add to a winning position, not a losing one.

Sun Tzu tells us

that to see victory when it is obvious is no sign of excellence or cleverness. To lift an autumn leaf requires no great strength, to see the sun and the moon does not indicate keen eyes, and to hear thunder does not necessitate sharp ears. Thus, good warriors win victories by not making mistakes and by positioning themselves where they will win.

We must think and anticipate and stay ahead of the crowd. Use the "what happens if" approach to your trading and investing. Develop a plan of action on the basis of an event or lack of an event. Again, you must learn to assess the big picture, anticipate strategic events, and bring that assessment down to a tactical and operational plan.

Sun Tzu reminds us ....

that the victorious army wins first and then seeks battle. A

wise leader rigorously adheres to method and discipline, and

thus it is in his power to control success.

Once you have analyzed the big picture and formed and developed your plan, it is imperative that you have the discipline to stick to it. It is a common mistake for traders to disobey their own rules. Doing so inevitably will lead to more lack of discipline and a series of losing trades.

Sun Tzu tells us ....
that the military has five rules: measurement, estimation, cal-
culation, balancing of chances, and victory.

Use your assessment of strategic conditions to determine where your market is now and where it could go (either up or down) given changes in those conditions. What is the potential risk to reward? How much of your capital are you willing to risk? What is the best use of your capital? Know when to enter a trade, and more important, know when to exit.

Sun Tzu concludes ···

this lesson by telling us that a victorious army as opposed to a routed one is like a pound on a scale with a grain. It is like a flood of water flowing into a deep chasm.

If you plan your trade and execute it properly, eventually it will become obvious to the less learned and the crowd will chase the market. Weak opposing trades will quickly capitulate and help drive the market and you to victory.

CHAPTER FIVE

EFFECTIVENESS

SEIZING OPPORTUNITIES

Sun Tzu said ....

that controlling a large force involves the same principle as
controlling a small one. Just divide their numbers. When in
battle, confront directly; victory is gained by surprise.

Control depends on your point of view. In years gone by, the major central banks of the world did not have as much power as the market did when they tried to intervene in the currency markets. The year 1995 brought a different tactic. It seemed as though the banks had learned their lesson. With the U.S. dollar trading at all-time lows against the yen, deutsche mark, Swiss franc, and many other currencies, the banks intervened at times when it was unexpected and when trading was unusually light: during Asian trading hours or long holiday weekends in the United States or in Europe. When the news hit and the market started to trade, they intensified their attack. Those who were short U.S. dollars scrambled to cover their positions, driving the market even further. The central banks accomplished what they had heretofore been unable to do.

As Sun Tzu said further: Be unorthodox, infinite, and inexhaustible.

$Sun\ Tzu\ said$ ....

as a log or stone rolls down a hill, good soldiers seek effectiveness from momentum.

Traders or investors can benefit as a market gains momentum, like a stone rolling down a hill. They can push it along by adding to their position of strength. For example, in the U.S. stock market, as more and more people try to pick a top to it, and some even sell stocks short, buyers come in and give support to prices. Eventually the buyers will move prices higher, causing the short sellers to buy back stocks, which drives the market up even more. Additionally, there are people sitting on the sidelines who don't want to be left behind, so they start buying. This cycle will repeat itself time and again, creating a market that is feeding on itself—like the log rolling down hill.

Sun Tzu said ....

that energy can be likened to the bending of a bow; decision,
to letting the arrow fly. Good fighters are swift and precise and
move opponents with the prospect of gain.

Once you have established your plan of attack, do not hesitate to execute the trade. Once you have established your position, let the market push you along. Let the weak longs or shorts get flushed out in their panic. Keep offering them a little at progressively better prices to you. When you sense capitulation, unleash the balance of your position with market orders.

CHAPTER SIX

FRAGILITY AND ABILITY

IDENTIFYING WHEN TO ATTACK AND WHEN TO RETREAT

Sun Tzu said ....

that those who are first on the field of battle will be rested and

those who follow will be exhausted. Good soldiers will cause

others to come to them.

If you establish your position early on, even if it means scaling in, you will not have to chase the market. You will be able to choose your entry points and timing. Those who follow the market will find that they will have to chase it, and thus will help drive your position. Let the market come to you. Sell the peaks or buy the dips.

Sun Tzu said

to appear at points which the enemy must hasten to defend.

March swiftly to places where you are not expected.

The unexpected largely depends on your perspective. How often have you seen a gap opening up or down? Sometimes following a day when a large move has taken place, the market goes even further the next day until the weak longs or shorts have capitulated, then it promptly goes back to where it was. This is called the "fade." Particularly in futures trading, market makers and locals will "fade" the market to flush out small traders so they can take the other side. Then they will bring the market back to where it was. For the individual trader, it is wise to recognize a fade and thus take advantage of the situation.

Sun Tzu tells us ....

to be extremely secretive, to be subtle and mysterious in our

battle plans.

No traders worth their salt will tell you what they are going to do. They will tell you after their position is on so you can spread the word and help drive the market. Another tactic of the major players is to advertise one position while they take the other side so they can liquidate their holdings.

Do you remember when a well-known hedge-fund operator gave a speech in Tokyo and told the world to sell yen and buy U.S. treasuries? Over the next month yen went up versus the U.S. dollar, while U.S. treasuries went down considerably. Do you suppose he needed the volume to liquidate his opposite positions? This was the beginning of the unwinding of the "borrow yen in Japan and buy U.S. treasuries" arbitrage trade.

Sun Tzu tells us ....

that to advance we should push though the enemy's weak

points: to retire we must be more rapid than the enemy.

One technique used by traders on the exchange floor is to "uptick" a rising market or "downtick" a falling one. This means that instead of buying the bid and selling the offer, they do the opposite and sell the bid and buy the offer. The result is to magnify a move in the market and help drive out weak opposing positions. Given the competition among market makers, you can try using limit orders. If you want to exit a position quickly, use market orders and get out fast.

Sun Tzu tells us ....

to awaken our enemies to find out where they are active and

where they are not. We must force them to reveal themselves

so as to discover where they are abundant and where they are

lacking.

For futures traders, the *Commitment of Traders* report can be very useful. Even more helpful is to watch the subsequent open interest and volume. What are the commercial interests doing as well as the large traders? It is fascinating that they are quite often on opposing sides. Position yourself to take advantage of a move.

How easily can you execute a limit order away from the market? If it is too easy, it could be you made a mistake. Did you get a particularly good fill on a market order? Again, you had better reevaluate your position.

Sun Tzu said

that warfare is fluid. It changes continuously, just as water will adapt its form to the earth. He who can change tactics in relation to his enemy or opponent will succeed in winning.

Markets change continuously and so must you. What worked last year, last month, or even last week may very well not work today. You must constantly test your methods to see if they are valid. You must consistently evaluate your thinking and assumptions to see if they still apply.

Sun Tzu concludes ....

this lesson by reminding us that he who can change tactics

relative to his opponent shows rare acumen.

Indeed, if you have the ability to change your thinking and tactics to respond to the market's changing, you will find yourself a consistent winner.

CHAPTER SEVEN

MANEUVERING

MANAGING
YOUR POSITION

Sun Tzu said ....

that the most difficult task of all was to maneuver an army; to

do so effectively, you must use deception and change the

enemy's perception of what you intend to do.

This advice is particularly useful for major market participants. Individual traders, too, need to recognize when they are being manipulated or being fed misinformation or disinformation.

Suppose you are a large, well-known market participant. You have taken advantage of an arbitrage opportunity by borrowing yen in Japan and using them to buy U.S. dollar-denominated bonds. Your analysis suggests that this opportunity has played itself out and now you want to liquidate your position. What do you do? Knowing that whatever you say will be picked up in the financial press, you espouse a strong dollar against the yen and likewise the benefits of owning U.S. bonds. You now have the volume necessary to liquidate your position and not upset the market in the process.

Sun Tzu said ....

that you cannot enter into alliances unless you know the

plans of your neighbors.

Given the preceding scenario, anticipate what the major market participants might do and form an alliance of other traders you can trust.

Sun Tzu said ....

that we cannot turn natural advantages to our benefit unless

we use local guides.

Do not hesitate to talk with your alliance and others who might have an informed opinion. Informed opinion does not mean inside information. It is difficult to trade from prison.

Sun Tzu tells us ....

to think about and consider our intended action and to keep

our plans secret: but when we move, to strike like a bolt of

lightning.

Once you have made your assessment and developed a plan, execute your trade. Do not hesitate to pull the trigger.

Sun Tzu reminds us ....

that a soldier's energy is keenest in the morning, by midday it

is on the wane, and at evening it just wants to return home.

Morning markets are the most active and the most liquid. They are largely public. Midday markets are thin and quiet. Most markets get more active and liquid in the afternoon prior to the close, but the activity is largely institutional.

Whom do you prefer to trade with? It is better to trade in a liquid market with good volume and to avoid midday markets, which are particularly thin and hazardous to your equity.

Sun Tzu tells us .... to exercise discipline and calm, to await the weary, disordered enemy. This is the art of mastering strength.

I would charge you to use proper money and risk management so that you are not a weak long or short. Patience is very difficult for most traders and investors. You must have the patience to wait for the proper time to execute your trade. You must exercise patience when your trade is working for you and not take that profit too soon.

$Sun\ Tzu\ urges\ us$ ....

to not attack an enemy whose ranks are in perfect order and

not to advance uphill.

How many times have you fought the tape? The axiom is that the trend is your friend. Hardly new advice but still as valid as ever.

CHAPTER EIGHT

VERSATILITY

DO NOT BE A ONE-WAY TRADER

Sun Tzu teaches ....

that when you are in difficult country, do not make camp. Do not stay in dangerous or isolated positions. You will find yourself in a desperate position and will have to fight.

Sun Tzu also says there are roads not to be followed and armies not to be attacked.

Sage advice for the small, inexperienced, or individual trader or investor. If you are a stock market or bond market investor, it would be a disaster for you to participate in the futures market without proper schooling. You would be entering a conflict in which you were clearly over your head. Even if you are an equity futures market trader, it would be a mistake for you to start trading currencies because the rules of engagement are different.

It is imperative that you adhere to the market you know.

Sun Tzu tells us ....

to not follow a pretended retreat.

How many times have you put on a trade and gotten flushed out by a small countermove—only to see the market go right back to where it was and then reach where you thought it might go? Beware the small counter move.

Discipline and planning are necessary to pick your entry point and, more important, your exit point or target. It is also necessary to know when you are wrong.

Sun Tzu tells us ....

that wise generals are versatile. The general who can easily

adapt will know how to employ his forces. The general who

does not, will not be able to take advantage of opportunities.

This chapter began with a familiar adage among traders: Do not be a one-way trader. Be as willing to sell as you are to buy. The general public is usually unwilling to sell and does so only out of desperation and fear. Professional traders, on the other hand, are usually very willing to sell short, since prices usually decline much more quickly than they advance.

It would be irresponsible of me to tell an average investor to start selling short. At the same time, it would benefit that average investor to be aware of this strategy and to recognize an opportunity when it arises.

Sun Tzu tells us ....

that the intelligent always consider both benefit and harm.

Carefully measure your risk and potential reward. Is the reward worth the risk? Is your capital better used elsewhere? For me, a risk-reward ratio of one to one is not worth it. I prefer to see three to one.

Sun Tzu tells us ....

there are five dangerous faults in generals: carelessness,

timidity, a quick temper, fragility, and overconcern for troops.

These faults can be found in many traders and investors as well. Do not be careless or reckless with your trading. You trade for profit, not for fun and games. Do not be timid; once you have identified an opportunity, attack. Act on it. Do not get angry over a losing trade and swear to get even. You won't. Do not get down on yourself for a losing trade, or even a string of losing trades. Find out what you are doing wrong and correct the problem. Do not fall in love with a stock, a bond, or anything else. You must learn that this is conflict, and you must be rather mercenary with your trading and investing.

CHAPTER NINE

STRATAGEM

POSITIONING YOURSELF

Sun Tzu said ....

that when you seek to establish a post for your army, position

yourself in high places so that you may observe the enemy.

In this era of 24-hour markets, instant access to information, and the global nature of our economy, it is imperative that you take other, related markets into account.

For example, if during the Asian trading session the Bank of Japan intervenes to sell yen and buy U.S. dollars, what effect will the move have on the U.S. fixed-income markets? Given that, what will the effect be on the U.S. stock market? If yen decline relative to U.S. dollars, what will the Japanese stock market do and what will the effect be on their banks' capital? If their capital declines, they might have to sell assets. What assets might they sell? Perhaps U.S. bonds? The idea is to think ahead and position yourself to take advantage of these events.

Sun Tzu advises us ....

to not fight in a river.

Do not try to trade a market in a tight range. You stand a better chance of victory if you wait until the market tips its hand.

Consider the S&P 500 futures market. Let's suppose it is a quiet day and the market is trading between 740 and 742. This is a floor trader's dream. If you are on the floor, you can see selling stop around 740, so you buy. Conversely, you can see buying stop around 742, so you sell. For those who are not on the floor, this is a very tough and treacherous market to trade in. To put on a trade inside that range, you are just placing a bet. The odds are you will get chopped to pieces. If, on the other hand, you wait until the market penetrates either side of that range, your odds of winning become considerably greater.

Sun Tzu tells us ....
to seek dry, flat country to confront the enemy.

Sun Tzu also urges us to take care of our soldiers. If we make
camp on solid ground, the army will be free of sickness and
we will ensure victory.

Your best liquidity is in the midprice range of the day. This is where most of the order flow is and where your best order fills will occur. The volume and price distribution on a normal day will look like a standard bell curve. There are days that will have two or three bells, however. These are the days of dramatic price moves that precipitate panic buying or selling.

Be mindful of your account equity. Choose your battles wisely and you will be successful.

Sun Tzu advises us ....

that when it rains upstream, it is best to wait until the swell

subsides before crossing.

As a small or individual trader, have you ever tried to trade in a late-afternoon market? Particularly in futures? You may well have found yourself in over your head.

Although I mentioned late afternoon, a flooded market condition can and does occur any time events warrant it. The rush of orders, particularly from major market participants, is so great that if you are on the wrong side, you literally cannot get out of the way fast enough. When this happens, it is better to stand aside and live to fight another day.

Sun Tzu advises ....

that when traveling over difficult ground, watch for a surprise

attack.

I never trade at midday or in a quiet market. It is a great place to be ambushed.

$\mathsf{Sun\ Tzu\ said}$ ....

that if the enemy sees ground or position to be gained but

does not act, it is weak.

Beware the price move without the volume and open interest from others to back it up. Low or weak volume price moves are suspect.

$Sun\ Tzu$ tells us ....

that the general who does not think ahead and takes his adversaries lightly will end up being their captive.

You must think ahead, plan your actions, and have the discipline to adhere to your plan. Never, ever underestimate what the market can do.

Sun Tzu concludes ....

this lesson by reminding us that if a general has confidence in his soldiers and his orders are obeyed, all will gain.

If you employ sound strategy, discipline, and good execution, your plan will be successful.

CHAPTER TEN

TERRAIN

KNOWING THE MARKET AND YOURSELF

Sun Tzu tells us ....

there are six types of terrain: accessible, entangling, temporizing, narrow passes, precipitous heights, and ground at a great distance.

Sun Tzu adds that accessible ground is that which can be freely traversed by both sides. We should establish a strong position first on the high and sunny side.

For you as a trader, this means staying with liquid markets, particularly if your means are limited. Then, once you have formed your plan and trade, get in early before the crowd recognizes what is happening.

Sun Tzu said

that entangling ground is that which is abandoned and is hard to reoccupy. If your enemies are unprepared, you may defeat them. If the enemy is ready for you and you fail to defeat, disaster will ensue.

For the trader, entangling ground is the light-volume day with erratic price swings. If you enter this market, you may find yourself in a position of having to withdraw or get out of a trade by chasing a countermove. Limit orders will not work, because you keep getting pushed back even further.

Sun Tzu said ....

that on temporizing ground, neither side will gain by making

the first move. Even if the other side shows attractive bait, it

is best to retreat.

This concept is particularly true in the futures markets. If a market has a large move up, the next day market makers will open it even higher to flush out weak shorts. Once the panic buying subsides, they will then take it lower. The opposite pattern holds after a large down day. Beware the "fade."

Sun Tzu said ....

that in narrow passes, you should occupy first with a strong

garrison. If the enemy is there first, withdraw and do not

attack.

Nothing goes up or down forever. After a sustained move in either direction, markets will enter a protracted period of narrow range trading and consolidate. In the futures market this gives us two options: You can direct your attention elsewhere for other opportunities, or you can watch the commitment of traders and open interest for clues as to who is taking positions.

Sun Tzu said ....

that on precipitous heights, occupy the high and sunny places
and await the enemy.

Most nonprofessional traders and investors wait until they feel safe before buying or selling anything. Then they chase the market. This is one of the foremost arguments for getting in early. When they do start to chase the market, use that opportunity to liquidate your position.

Sun Tzu said ....

that for ground at a great distance, it is difficult to provoke

battle and that doing so will work to your disadvantage.

This is the narrow, quiet, choppy, range-bound market in which commercial interests have no interest to buy or to sell. Save your resources for another opportunity.

Sun Tzu counsels

that there are six faults of generals that lead to defeat: flight, insubordination, collapse, ruin, disorganization, and rout.

Sun Tzu also said that if one force is hurled against another ten times its size, the result will be flight of the former.

Those who are overtrading (trading too much) or taking positions too large for their means will fall prey to a larger force. The result is that they will be "trading scared," and thus have a weak hand, and will get flushed out easily.

Sun Tzu said ....

that when the common soldier is strong and the officers are

weak, the result is insubordination.

Do not let your greed get the better of your judgment.

Sun Tzu said ....
that if the officers are strong and the common soldier is weak,
the result is collapse.

In your market analysis, do not get so cerebral that you are ineffective. It doesn't matter if the computer says so, reality is the last sale.

Traders and investors have a tendency to overanalyze. One of the stages every trader (and many investors) goes through is over-reliance on mechanical and computerized trading systems. These are very useful tools, but they are not answers. Many times I have seen the technical indicators say, "sell," yet the market just refuses to cooperate. It keeps on trading up. The only truth is the last sale. Fight the tape and you will collapse.

Sun Tzu said

....

that when higher-ranking officers are angry and give battle on their own account out of resentment, before the general can assess whether he is in a position to fight, the result is ruin.

Sun Tzu further counsels that when the general is weak, lacks authority, has no clear orders, and ranks in a haphazard manner, the result is disorganization.

Do not enter trades too early out of desperation. These trades are inevitably losers born of rash thinking.

You must remain at all times consistent in the exercise of your trading plan, money management, and risk management. Failure to use discipline will lead to chaos.

Sun Tzu said ....

generals who are unable to estimate an enemy's strength, who

allow a weak force to engage a strong force, and who neglect

to place picked soldiers in the front rank will end up being

routed.

An analogy is to a stock investor getting prematurely involved in currency futures. The rules of engagement are clearly different and in another league entirely.

Are you trading in a market or involved in a strategy that is clearly over your head? Do not let your ego get the better of your judgment.

Sun Tzu concludes

this lesson by telling us that an experienced soldier, once in motion, is never confused. Once camp is broken, he is never at a loss. Hence the saying: If you know the enemy and know yourself, your victory will never be in doubt; if you know Heaven and Earth, your victory will be complete.

Know your market; learn everything you can about it. Know yourself: your resources, your intellect, and your psychological qualities. Maintain the discipline of your plan and victory will be yours.

CHAPTER ELEVEN

NINE CIRCUMSTANCES

SURVIVAL TACTICS

Sun Tzu said

that in the art of war, there are nine types of ground: dispersive ground, facile ground, contentious ground, open ground, intersecting ground, serious ground, difficult ground, desperate ground, and hemmed-in ground.

For you as a trader or investor, this means recognizing the circumstance you find yourself and the market in, and choosing whether to do battle.

Sun Tzu said ....

dispersive ground is where local chieftains fight among themselves. Therefore, fight not.

A dispersive market typically occurs a day or two prior to a big economic report or expected event. It is usually characterized by periods of quiet followed by periods of very choppy price action and flurries of activity, as locals and market makers trade among themselves. To take positions in this type of market as a small or independent trader can be hazardous to your account equity.

Sun Tzu said ....

entering other's land but gaining no great distance is facile

ground. Therefore, halt not.

This is taking the small position. As it goes for you, add to it. If it does not, you can get out easily without much harm.

Trading or investing is about probabilities. Let's suppose you spot an opportunity. If you place a large order and are wrong, the results will be disastrous. If, on the other hand, you place a small order and are wrong, you can get out without much harm. If you place that small order and are correct in your assessment, you then add to it.

Professionals average up; amateurs average down.

Sun Tzu said ....

that ground which is of equal value to either side is con-

tentious ground. Therefore, attack not.

When large market participants are of opposing views, market activity is typically extremely volatile with high volume and large trades. It is quite risky for the small trader to get involved in this conflict.

Sun Tzu said

that ground on which each side can come and go easily is open ground. Therefore, do not attempt to block the enemy's way.

An open-ground market is a freely flowing market. Activity is good but price swings are smooth and go freely from support to resistance areas. This type of market is easy to trade in if you just go with the flow.

Sun Tzu said ....

that ground which forms the key to three states so that he

who occupies it first has command of the empire is intersect-

ing ground. Therefore, join hands with allies.

An intersecting market means something has to give. The market is searching for leadership. In equities, the leader will be a particular group of stocks. In debt, it will be a particular portion of the yield curve. In currencies, one in particular will lead the rest.

The stock market is a good example of this concept. A certain group of stocks—maybe consumer stocks, perhaps oil stocks, or old-fashioned "smoke stack" industrial stocks—starts to move first, before a move in the broad averages. Lately, high-tech stocks have led the market both up and down.

Debt is more subtle. Increasing yield spreads over treasuries on credit and finance corporate debt quite often precede an economic recession. You could therefore anticipate that event and start to position yourself accordingly.

Take small multiple positions in each. Then quickly build your position in one when the leader becomes evident.

Sun Tzu said

that when an army has penetrated deeply into another's territory, this is serious ground. Therefore, gather in plunder.

Let's say you have done everything right. You got in early, you added to your winning position, and now the market is really starting to panic and move even more in your direction. This is when you go for the throat. Add to your position, then keep offering to liquidate at better and better prices to you.

Sun Tzu said ....

that ground that includes mountains, forests, steep terrain,

and marshes is difficult ground.

This is the narrow, choppy, inside day. Best to leave it alone and not trade.

Sun Tzu said

that desperate ground is that on which you can be saved from defeat only by fighting quickly, without delay. Therefore, fight.

Desperate ground is for guerrilla traders. They go in for quick stabs and get out. This strategy is intended for the professional full-time trader and is particularly useful in fast-moving futures markets. Professionals trade stocks for a quarter point, bonds for thirty-seconds of a point, or currencies for small fractions of a yen or deutsche marks. It is not a viable scheme for average investors. They would be chewed to bits.

Sun Tzu said ....

that ground which you reach through narrow gorges and from which you can retire only by tortuous paths and be ambushed by a small force is hemmed-in ground. Therefore, resort to stratagem.

When you find yourself in one of those difficult situations, try not to panic. Think instead of a creative solution to your problem. This plight is more common among average investors than among professionals, although it happens to them as well.

I like to think that there is always something to do. Sometimes, the best avenue is one of escape. It is better to escape wounded than to die on the battlefield. Other times, it may be better to make use of kindred markets such as options, assuming you know what you are doing.

The point is not to panic. Stay calm and think your predicament though. Decide on a course of action. Once you have done that, execute your plan.

Sun Tzu said

that skillful leaders of old knew how to drive a wedge between the enemy's troops. They went into battle only when it was to their advantage to do so.

Trading is a business and you should treat it as such. If you see no advantage to entering a market, it is best to stand aside and wait for a better day and another opportunity.

Sun Tzu when asked .... how he coped with a large, well-organized force ready to attack, replied that he takes something which they hold dear.

It is well known among professionals that weak hands and small participants will get out of a position if it moves above or below the previous day's high or low. They will therefore take something which you hold dear. Knowing this, do not give it to them so easily.

$\mathsf{Sun\ Tzu\ said}$ ....

that the essence of war is rapidity—that is, taking advantage

of others who are not ready.

Once you spot an opportunity, do not hesitate to execute your trade. Take advantage of weak hands.

Sun Tzu said ....

that the further you penetrate into a hostile country, the greater

the solidarity of your troops. Thus, defenders will not prevail.

Once again, this is the concept of adding to a winning position with momentum on your side. It is even more true in the commodity futures markets, where losers have to be liquidated quickly, driving the market further.

Sun Tzu said

that when soldiers are in desperate straits, they lose their sense of fear. If there is no place of refuge, they will stand firm and show a stubborn front.

After a market moves a great distance, there will come a point when it will move no more. Make sure that you are aware of that spot and that someone is there to take the other side of your trade. Do not overstay in a market or try to cherry-pick the top or bottom.

Sun Tzu said ....

that the skillful tactician is like the Shuai-Jan, a snake found in the mountains. Strike at its head and you will be attacked by its tail. Strike at its tail and you will be attacked by its head. Strike at the middle and you will be attacked by both.

You should be flexible and not a one-way trader. Most people will risk their capital to buy something in the hope that it will rise in price, but they will not risk selling something short if the prospect is that it will decline in price. Certainly, selling short is not a strategy for the neophyte. Short sellers should be well experienced and aware of the risks involved. I need not tell you that experienced professional traders are more than willing to sell short, since prices generally decline much more rapidly than they advance.

You should learn to expect the unexpected. Think ahead about what it would take for something good or bad to happen. Then consider the outcome given each set of circumstances. Most important, have a plan in place to take advantage of each situation.

Sun Tzu when asked ....
if an army can be made to imitate the Shuai-Jan snake,
replied that it can.

You must not only be flexible. You must learn to anticipate the adversary, plan your response, and execute without hesitation.

The number *du jour* in recent times has been the monthly non-farm payroll. Bond prices can and do have violent reactions if this number is a surprise. To put a position on prior to its release is not trading, it's gambling. To be like the Shuai-Jan snake, you could have stop orders on both sides of the market, or you could use both puts and calls. In either case, once the number is released, sell the loser and add to the winner. Let the people that are wrong help drive your position. Exploit their weakness.

Sun Tzu said ....

that the business of the general is to be quiet and thus ensure secrecy and maintain order.

Be methodical in your trading plans. When a given economic report is due to come out, plan ahead of time what you will do if it is in line with expectations or if it is a surprise in either direction. Gauge what the likely market response will be.

Sun Tzu said ....

that the general keeps his soldiers and officers ignorant of

his plans.

As mentioned previously, no traders worth their salt are going to tell you what they plan to do. Every time I tune into those market "seers" on television, I wonder what their position is. If you have a good idea, keep it to yourself until you have established your position. Conversely be aware that, in pushing a position, others could just be promoting a trade they are already in.

The Internet and other on-line services have hundreds of chat rooms, message boards, news groups, and so forth. Besides being a regulatory nightmare for the government, these chat rooms, news groups, message boards, and so forth are either full of amateurs with enough knowledge to be dangerous, or other people hyping something to help drive a position they already have. Be very skeptical of what you read or hear.

The National Association of Security Dealer's Regulatory body (NASDR) has information that can help you. I would urge and encourage you to contact them.

Sun Tzu said ....

that the leader of an army should act like someone who

climbs up a height and then throws away the ladder.

Professional traders and those who want to be traders must focus, concentrate, and not be distracted.

Sun Tzu reminds us ....

that the different measures suited to the nine types of

ground—the expediency of offensive or defensive tactics—

must be studied, along with human nature.

You must learn not only the tactics involved in trading but market psychology as well. I have seen numerous computerized trading programs. I have examined all the historical technical tools. Nothing can replace an appreciation for market psychology and pure gut instinct.

Sun Tzu concludes ....

this lesson by admonishing us to lead an army as if it was a
single soldier. When in danger, a soldier will strive for victory.
He who focuses on the enemy can kill from a great distance.

Many traders will look at an opportunity and see only the risk or how badly they can be hurt. You must learn to see the reward side of the equation, to keep a single-minded purpose of winning and not be distracted from the task at hand.

CHAPTER TWELVE

FIRE ATTACK

AGGRESSIVE MOVES

Sun Tzu said ....

there are five kinds of attack by fire: to burn soldiers, to burn

stores of supplies, to burn baggage trains, to burn arsenals

and magazines, and to drop fire among the enemy.

This advice applies primarily to major market participants. Most small or independent traders are not capable of starting fires in the market, but it is well worth their while to learn not to get caught in a backdraft.

Sun Tzu said ....

that when fire is set inside a camp, respond quickly from the
outside.

When major dealers find themselves in lopsided positions—that is, owning too much or being caught short—other dealers who manage to find out will do their best to take advantage and exacerbate the situation. That is when the major players buy too dear or are willing to sell too cheaply.

Sun Tzu said ....

that if fire breaks out but the enemy's soldiers are quiet, bide

your time.

We might call this the art of the sandbag. It goes along with the concept of not following a false retreat. Dealers will try to show a false position to lure others into following it and then take the other side.

Sun Tzu said ....

that when the force of the flames has reached its height,

follow up with an attack if practicable; if not, stay where

you are.

If you have the resources to join the fray, by all means go for the throat. If not, stand aside.

In today's age of computerized trading, markets can get particularly volatile. For the small trader, to get involved is to invite disaster. Once panic buying or selling starts, it usually precipitates more of the same until a "capitulation" stage is reached. If you sense this and have the financial and electronic resources to participate, you may feel comfortable doing so. However, you had better be the cool, unemotional warrior that Sun Tzu counsels you must be.

Sun Tzu said ....

that if it is possible to make an assault with fire from without,

do not wait for it to break out within, but deliver your attack

at the right moment.

On occasion, the dealer community or locals in the futures markets will try to start a fire to see what the reaction is. The goal is to smoke out "weak hands" and potential buyers or sellers at a particular level.

This is admittedly a difficult situation for the small trader; short-lived, adverse price moves do not make them any less real. The only thing you can do is protect yourself with stop-loss orders and then reassess the situation.

Sun Tzu said ....

that when you start a fire, be to the windward of it, not the

leeward.

If you sense a fire starting, make sure you are upwind and not downwind. Whatever market you are involved in, when you sense it is about to move, there is only one thing to do: act, and act now. Get on the right side of the market or get out of the way. There is an old adage about not fighting the tape—and this is it.

Sun Tzu said ....

that the daytime wind lasts long but fails at night.

In this day and age, when is it night? We have three principal trading sessions: the Asian session, the European session, and the North American session. The dealer community's "book" gets passed from Tokyo to London to New York. This 24-hour trading session is more applicable in the debt and foreign exchange markets than in the equity markets. As a small or independent trader, you would be wise to limit your risk in this environment.

The currency market is the best example of this concept. The currency market is the largest market in the world; it dwarfs the stock market. It is also largely an institutional market. Quite often you will see large moves in prices in the Asian and European sessions, but when the market opens in the United States, prices will literally just sit there.

For the small trader to get involved in this market, it is better to use smaller positions or risk-limiting strategies.

Sun Tzu said

not to move unless you see an advantage, not to use troops unless there is something to be gained, and not to fight unless the position is critical.

As mentioned previously, you do not trade for fun and games. You trade to make money. Trading is a dangerous business, particularly in the more leveraged arenas of options and futures. You get paid to take risks, so do not commit your resources lightly.

Sun Tzu finishes

this lesson by reminding us to act only when it is to our benefit. A kingdom once destroyed cannot be brought back, nor can the dead be restored to life. This is the way to keep a country at peace and an army intact.

It is often said that the business of a trader is to stay in business. If you are frivolous in your methods, your equity will soon be gone and you will be out of business. So act when you see an opportunity and be content to stand aside when you do not.

CHAPTER THIRTEEN

COLLECTING INTELLIGENCE

CREATING YOUR NETWORK

Sun Tzu said ....

that what enables the wise sovereign and the good general to

achieve beyond the reach of ordinary men is foreknowledge,

and this knowledge must come from people.

We all know that in the securities markets, using inside information is patently illegal. This does not mean that you cannot form a network of other people, those you trust, to share thoughts, ideas, and strategies.

Sun Tzu said ....

that if a secret is heard before a spy reports it, the spy must be put to death.

Beware the secondhand rumor. It is illegal to spread rumors, but that doesn't mean it doesn't happen. I cannot tell you how often I have heard the same item of intelligence several times. Rumors almost always turn out to be false. Be careful not to act on false intelligence.

CONCLUSION

I said in the beginning of this text that Sun Tzu has changed the way I view the markets. You have noticed that there are no magic oscillators. No mystical technical indicators. What Sun Tzu teaches throughout *The Art of War* is taught to assess the opponent and the strategic situation, to be flexible and learn to adapt to an ever changing environment, and finally to employ tactical methods and know when to strike and when not to strike. Most of all, what Sun Tzu has taught me is to think clearly. I hope he has done the same for you.

ABOUT THE AUTHOR

Dean Lundell (Chicago, IL) has been in the securities business for more than 20 years. He is the principal of Osiris Trading Ltd., where he specializes in arbitrage and managed money trading in currencies and interest rate futures. His firm provides a daily market advisory letter and offers managed money services.

Before forming Osiris Trading, Lundell was a vice president at Merrill Lynch Capital Markets. He was also a principal of Crestar Investment Bank, and is a licensed commodity trading advisor and commodity pool operator. A veteran of the Vietnam War, Lundell knows battle firsthand and is uniquely qualified to apply Sun Tzu's time-tested military principles to winning in financial markets. "Sun Tzu said that the general who follows these principles will be victorious," writes Lundell. "And so shall you."

For more information on applying Sun Tzu's Art of War to the art of trading, visit www.artofwar.com.